Series / Number 04-018

Political Beliefs about the Structure of Government: Congress and the Presidency

GLENN R. PARKER
Miami University

 **SAGE PUBLICATIONS** / **Beverly Hills** / **London**

For information address:

SAGE PUBLICATIONS, INC.
275 South Beverly Drive
Beverly Hills, California 90212

SAGE PUBLICATIONS, LTD.
St George's House / 44 Hatton Garden
London EC1N 8ER

International Standard Book Number 0-8039-0461-4

Library of Congress Catalog Card No. 74-81082

FIRST PRINTING

When citing a professional paper, please use the proper form. Remember to cite the
correct Sage Professional Paper series title and include the paper number. One of the
two following formats can be adapted (depending on the style manual used):

(1) NAGEL, S. S. (1973) "Comparing Elected and Appointed Judicial Systems."
Sage Professional Papers in American Politics, 1, 04-001. Beverly Hills and London:
Sage Pubns.

OR

(2) Nagel, Stuart S. 1973. *Comparing Elected and Appointed Judicial Systems.* Sage
Professional Papers in American Politics, vol. 1, no. 04-001. Beverly Hills and
London: Sage Publications.

CONTENTS

Political Beliefs about the Structure of Government: Congress and the Presidency

GLENN R. PARKER
Miami University

INTRODUCTION

Even ignoring the serious institutional confrontations arising from the investigation of the burglary at the Democratic National Headquarters during the 1972 Election, the long awaited crisis in legislative-executive relations would still be at hand. The progressive attrition of legislative influence has, for some time, occupied the attention of political analysts. Legislators themselves have frequently lamented their fallen estate, even as they have heralded presidential initiatives and have granted more flexibility to the executive branch. Obviously, conflicts between Congress and the President are not novel, having been assured by the actions of the Founding Fathers; what is unusual, however, is the extensive acrimony surrounding present confrontations between the legislative and executive branches. These conflicts appear especially acute in the area of domestic policy where the President has launched an attack on the panoply of New-Deal-to-Great-Society programs which have blossomed and matured over the past 30 years.

A variety of techniques have been utilized by both political institutions in such legislative-executive clashes—Senate confirmation of presidential appointments, congressional investigation, presidential veto, General Account-

AUTHOR'S NOTE: *I would like to express my indebtedness to Roger H. Davidson, who, in addition to making available the data upon which this analysis is based, provided numerous helpful suggestions throughout the entire inquiry. The paper has also benefited from the advice and comments of Thomas E. Cronin, Donald J.*

ing Office audits. Yet, perhaps, the most potent weapon may be the standing of the President with the American public (James, 1969: 115).

"The prevalent impression of a President's public standing," writes Richard Neustadt (1961: 87), "tends to set a tone and define the limits of what Washingtonians do for him or do to him." The linkage between public opinion and presidential action is, however, extremely difficult to establish; there are far too many instances of unpopular presidential measures. Nevertheless, the lack of public support appears to place a drain on presidential power:

> He may not be left helpless, but his options are reduced, his opportunities diminished, his freedom for maneuver checked in the degree that Washington conceives him unimpressive to the public [Neustadt, 1961: 90].

In a similar manner, Elmer Cornwell (1966: 4) speaks of popular support of the Chief Executive as the "very essence of the power to influence the process of governance." And Louis Koenig (1964: 182) suggests that the capacity of the President to summon broad public support is "his most substantial means of bringing Congress around to an accommodation productive of policy and action." There seems little doubt that whenever the President is able to mobilize a substantial segment of the public to his side "he is a truly formidable figure" (McConnell, 1967: 74).

The nature of the presidential- and congressional-support publics (e.g., size, capacity for mobilization, basis of attachment) could influence mass response to institutional pleas for popular support. For instance, if attachment to Congress is due to its historical heritage of political conservatism then a Congress which is significantly more liberal than the man in the White House, as appears to be the case with President Nixon and the 93rd Congress, would find it more difficult to mobilize its supporters; if support for a political institution is passive, it would be even more difficult to mobilize. Moreover, if support for Congress and the President were wedded to the current popularity of the two institutions, congressional and presi-

Devine, and Marvin G. Weinbaum, all of whom read earlier drafts of various sections of this manuscript. None of the above individuals, however, bear any responsibility for the interpretations presented here. This analysis is the product of a larger study of mass orientations toward Congress which is supported by a grant from the Committee on Governmental and Legal Processes of the Social Science Research Council. An earlier version of this paper was presented at the 1973 Annual Meeting of the American Political Science Association, Jung Hotel, New Orleans, Louisiana, September 4-8, 1973.

dential supporters could be prone to "switch" loyalties, creating a floating, rather than a stable, base of political support.

This paper seeks to explore the nature of the institutional constituencies which provide the basic support for the legislative and executive branches of the national government. It employs the term "constituency" in one of its less common usages—namely, as defining a body of supporters. The analysis will present some preliminary findings on the presidential- and congressional-support publics by examining the characteristics, attitudes, and political involvements of those who express a distinct preference for either legislative or executive leadership in the formation of public policy.

Prior to this phase of the inquiry, however, we will describe some attitudinal supports upon which the political structures can draw.[1] For this segment of the study, we will include attitudes toward the Supreme Court, and thereby, provide an additional standard for evaluating institutional orientations toward Congress and the President. In the following sections, then, we shall seek to characterize some aspects of the attitudinal environment which surround the legislative and executive branches of government.

SALIENCY

The general lack of popular interest in political institutions seems to be a well-ingrained feature of our political system. The Supreme Court appears to be especially unlikely to capture the attention of the mass public. A 1966 national survey shows that a majority of the populace is unable to recall anything the Supreme Court has recently done which they like or dislike; a similar proportion is unable to name a single Supreme Court Justice (Murphy and Tanenhaus, 1969: 549). Moreover, in separate studies, Kenneth Dolbeare (1967), and Walter Murphy and Joseph Tanenhaus (1968) report that only a partial recognition of Supreme Court decisions concerning reapportionment exists among the citizenry—even where redistricting has occurred. Murphy and Tanenhaus (1968: 363) suggest that such a limited issue awareness results from the fact that people cannot relate reapportionment to their daily lives. Dolbeare (1967: 194) indicates that the same is true in Wisconsin for the criminal procedure cases, which had been subject to open attack through the state: "Perhaps defendant's rights issues," he comments, "are the private reserve of policemen and editorial writers."

Public attention to Congress appears to be no more extensive. We observe, for example, that less than half of the populace can name their representative (43 percent); about four in five are unaware of their congressman's vote on a single issue (81 percent); less than a third know when their representative must next "stand" for election (30 percent).[2] There is good reason to believe, however, that the presidency has attained a higher level of saliency than either Congress or the Supreme Court.

Although little information is available on the saliency of the Chief Executive, it is widely accepted that the President is a prominent and important symbol of political authority in early childhood—a critical period in the formation of political and institutional orientations. Indeed, a number of children appear to consider legislators as little more than "the President's helpers" (Greenstein, 1965: 62). It is no wonder, then, that the legislative and judicial branches of the national government are not viewed as very significant elements of the political framework (Easton and Dennis, 1969: 149).

The greater importance of the Chief Executive during adolescence, vis-a-vis Congress and the Court, is likely to contribute to the saliency of the President in later adult life. Moreover, media concentration on presidential politics further bolsters the saliency of the President (Cornwell, 1959: 279-280). The following data suggest the magnitude of the success of the presidency in dominating the attention of the American public.

Thus, it appears that the presidency is, by far, the most salient institution; the Supreme Court is the least salient, with Congress holding the medial position (Table 1). One particularly interesting consequence of the ranking operation is that it reflects the readiness of the American populace to differentiate between the three branches of the federal government. More than three-quarters of our sample (77 percent) provide complete preference rankings. We are, therefore, led to conclude that for the vast majority of the public, the political institutions of the national government can be arranged and distinguished in terms of their imputed saliency for the individual.

What is most noticeable about these preference orderings is the large amount of variation in saliency among the political structures; there is little question as to which institution is the first, second, or even last among "equals." We observe, for instance, that less than a third of the sample is most attentive to the actions of Congress or the Supreme Court; moreover, approximately 8 of every 10 specify the Supreme Court as the institution which they follow "least closely." Clearly, although some of our respondents place congressional affairs above the activities of the Chief Executive or the Supreme Court, Congress is ill-adapted to vie with the President for the attention of the American public. Despite the relative

Table 1.

RANK ORDER DISTRIBUTIONS FOR THE SALIENCY OF
CONGRESS, THE PRESIDENCY, AND THE SUPREME COURT[a]

| | Saliency Rank | | | | |
Institution	First	Second	Third	Percent[b]	N
Congress	23%	58%	18%	99	3154
Presidency	69	26	5	100	3154
Supreme Court	8	16	77	101	3154
Percent	100%	100%	100%		
N=	3154	3154	3154		

a. The following items are utilized in measuring levels of institutional saliency:

> Thinking now of the three branches of the national government
> in Washington--the Presidency, the Congress, and the Supreme
> Court--which one do you follow most closely?

> Which do you follow least closely--the Presidency, the Congress,
> or the Supreme Court?

These two items determine the respondent's first and last (third)
ranks; the "residual" institution automatically occupies the
second rank.

b. Total percentages do not equal 100% due to rounding. Cases
involving tied ranks or missing data have been deleted in this
table.

SOURCE: Comparative State Elections Project, University of North
Carolina.

lack of saliency of Congress and the Court, the impact which these institutions have on an individual's life does not go unnoticed.

IMPACT

To be considered important, a governmental structure must not only be attended to, but must also be recognized as having significant effects upon the lives of individual citizens. Political scientists, and others who write and think extensively about politics, tend to assume that government has a direct, inescapable effect upon the lives of all citizens. This is not entirely true, even in the abstract. Certainly the effects of governmental performance are not perceived equally by everyone. A very large number of citizens live out their lives with little thought to the ways in which the government inpinges upon their activities. For many people, this may simply reflect ignorance of the workings of government, or diversion caused by the concrete activities of daily existence. Other persons may minimize the impact of government as a rationalization for intense antipathies toward governmental policies. Although we cannot always determine which motivation dominates, in either case the person would attribute slight impact to government actions.

Citizens tend to agree with textbook pronouncements that the institutions of the national government directly affect their lives. Interestingly, citizens are more inclined to testify that Congress has a "great effect" upon their lives than to express the same view concerning the President or the Court (Table 2). This slight advantage in the perceived effects of Congress is especially difficult to explain in light of several factors which seem to favor the presidency, including the importance of the Chief Executive in the legislative arena—an extremely visible governmental output:

> The initiative in formulating legislation, in assigning legislative, priorities, in arousing support for legislation, and in determining the final content of the legislation enacted has clearly shifted to the executive branch—President, administration, and bureaucracy—have gained legislative functions at the expense of Congress [Huntington, 1965: 23].

Moreover, the factors which seem to favor the presidency would also tend to have a diluting effect on perceptions of the impact of congressional performance. The organizational design of Congress, for one thing, makes legislative affairs difficult to fathom for the typical citizen and may therefore invite the conclusion that Congress makes a negligible contribution in the governing of the polity.

Perhaps more importantly, the actions of Congress are likely to bypass an individual's attention span. In addition to the lack of interest which politics stirs within the mass public, the relative lack of "congressional news" further restricts the information available about the activities of Congress. A good illustration of the scarcity of information concerning Congress is provided by the research experiences of the staff of the Survey Research Center of the University of Michigan:

> In 1958, when there was no presidential ballyhoo to occupy newspaper space, we initiated an analysis of newspaper content relating to local congressional candidates campaigning for re-election. The project was rapidly dropped because examination of newspapers even after the campaign was well under way showed that information about such candidates was printed only sporadically and then was usually buried in such a remote section of the paper that the item would go unheeded by all but the more avid readers of political news [Converse, 1962: 586].

Furthermore, partly as a result of media concentration on presidential affairs, in lieu of legislative politics, people are unlikely to focus whatever limited attention they do direct at political matters to congressional affairs; hence a distorted image of the impact of Congress is likely to be implanted upon an individual's cognitive map of the political world. The importance which attention to legislative politics has on perceptions of the impact of Congress is clearly illustrated by Table 3. Thus, lack of attention to congressional affairs depresses the impact attributed to the actions of Congress. Yet, despite the relative lack of saliency, Congress maintains a slight lead over the presidency in the area of perceived impact.

One explanation for the apparent paradox of the congressional advantage in perceived effect may rest on the fact that while the executive branch has assumed a more active, if not dominant role, in legislative decision-making, the populace continues to view Congress as the institution primarily responsible for lawmaking—the most visible result of governmental action (Lane, 1962: 147-148). Thus, although Congress may have lost ground in its battle with the presidency to retain legislative supremacy, the public may still view the legislature as the primary lawmaking sector of the national government; the slightly greater impact attributed to legislative action may be a response to the assumed dominance of Congress in policy-making, the governmental activity of which people are most cognizant.

Table 2.

THE IMPACT OF CONGRESS, THE PRESIDENCY

AND THE SUPREME COURT[a]

Assessment	Congress	Presidency	Supreme Court
Great Effect	45%	34%	31%
Some Effect	53	57	57
No Effect	5	9	12
Percent[b]	101%	100%	100%
N=	3903	3946	3751

a. The following items are utilized in measuring levels of institu-
    tional impact:

    Thinking now about the work of the President, about how much
    effect do you think his activities--the work he does, the
    speeches he makes, and so on--have on your day-to-day life?

    What about the Congress in Washington? How much effect do
    you think its activities--the laws it passes, and so on--has
    on your day-to-day life?

    Also, the Supreme Court in Washington? About how much effect
    do you think its decisions have on your day-to-day life?

b. Total percentages do not equal 100% due to rounding.

SOURCE: Comparative State Elections Project, University of North
         Carolina.

Table 3.

ATTENTION TO CONGRESSIONAL AFFAIRS

AND PERCEPTIONS OF THE IMPACT OF CONGRESS

	Saliency Rank of Congress		
Impact	Third	Second	First
Great Effect	35%	41%	58%
Some Effect	54	55	39
No Effect	11	4	3
	100%	100%	100%

Gamma = .28

SOURCE: Comparative State Elections Project, University of North Carolina.

We would like to point out that the perceived impact of the presidency is virtually identical to the impact ascribed to the Supreme Court, despite the fact that "there may be only a few jurisdictions in which a Court decision, even a doctrinally important one, can have a specific effect on individuals" (Wasby, 1970: 39). Perhaps contemporary Supreme Court decisions on issues controversial in nature and with far-reaching implications, such as school integration, have increased the public's awareness of the impact of the Court. In sum, there appears to be a substantial recognition on the part of the American public that the performance of political institutions affects their everyday lives; yet, individuals are more likely to attribute a slightly greater impact to congressional, in contrast to presidential or Supreme Court, action. Apparently, citizens do not appreciate as yet the scholarly literature that acknowledges the President as the chief legislator.

CONFIDENCE

Citizen trust in government has experienced considerable decline during the last decade (Miller, 1972), and the political institutions of the federal government have not been spared from this collapse in popular confidence. According to Louis Harris (1972), "public confidence in the leaders of both public and private institutions continues at a low ebb." Harris observes that less than three of every ten respondents expresses a "great deal" of confidence in those in charge of running Congress, the Executive, or the Supreme Court. Yet, people are apt to differentiate among the three branches of the national government with respect to institutional trust. More than 60 percent of our respondents provide complete preference orderings. Although the proportion of the sample willing to distinguish among the political institutions of the federal government in terms of confidence is less than occurred with respect to institutional saliency (77 percent in this latter instance), this subset represents a sizeable proportion of the entire sample. Therefore, we feel justified in concluding that for the vast majority of the populace, the political institutions of the national government can be distinguished on the basis of the amount of faith and confidence their actions instill.

The discrepancy in the sample proportions which are capable of discriminating among the political institutions with respect to saliency and confidence may be due to the fact that confidence contains a more explicit affective component than does saliency. Thus, it may be exceedingly more difficult to distinguish among political structures where *feelings* toward the institution are at issue, than where concern is with the allocation of one's attention span (saliency). Other studies of institutional orientations have reported a similar reluctance on the part of respondents to express, in terms of confidence or trust, an institutional preference; for instance, in 1966, more than a third of the populace declined to distinguish between their trust in the Supreme Court and their trust in Congress (Murphy and Tanenhaus, 1969: 551).

There is some evidence on institutional confidence which strongly suggests that the public has greater trust in the performance of the President than in the actions of Congress; and, slightly greater faith in the actions of Congress, vis-a-vis the Supreme Court (Murphy and Tanenhaus, 1969: 551). In her study of the public's image of the President, Roberta Sigel (1966: 127) notes that one-half of those interviewed preferred presidential leadership to that supplied by a consolidation of public and congressional stewardship: "Whatever doubts our sample had with regard to the wisdom of granting a president much power does not stem from lack of faith in the president's dedication to the public interest." Similarly, Thomas Cronin's (1970) analysis of trust in the presidency, the Senate, and the Supreme Court suggests that the public is most likely to believe that the President could "be trusted to do what is good for the people."

A contrasting perspective is provided by Kenneth Dolbeare (1967: 197), who concludes that the public has a greater trust in congressional, as compared to presidential, action. In order to ascertain the public's relative confidence in the institutions of the national government, Dolbeare asks respondents whether they "would be likely to think the right thing had been done in Washington if the action had been taken by the Supreme Court (President, Congress)?" The author observes that a third of his sample refused to attribute correctness to presidential action—a group that is twice as large as the number who would deny correctness to legislative action (16 percent).

Our findings tend to be somewhat more equivocal on the issue of which institution—Congress or the presidency—generates the greatest public confidence: Faith in the federal government is evenly distributed between Congress and the President (Table 4).[3] The differences between the frequency with which Congress or the presidency is ranked first or second in terms of institutional trust are of such slight magnitude that they must be viewed as being of rather insignificant discriminatory value. Perhaps the most notable feature of Table 4 is the general lack of faith in the actions of the Supreme Court. Here our findings are not uncertain—three of every four respondents select the Supreme Court as the political structure of the national government in whose actions they have the least amount of confidence. Thus, despite the aura of sanctity which is commonly assumed to surround the Court, the populace appears to have considerably more faith in the performances of Congress or the President. This conclusion is consistent with an earlier observation by Walter Murphy and Joseph Tanenhaus (1969: 552) that "a majority of the adult population that has an opinion has greater trust in Congress than in the Supreme Court."

The relative lack of confidence in the performance of the Supreme Court may be due to the fact that since its members are not subject to the same electoral fortunes as Congress or the President, the institution is viewed as less capable of being held accountable for its actions. The increased unpopularity of various Supreme Court decisions, like school busing, may further foster the conviction that the Court is isolated from public opinion and, therefore, citizen control. In sum, although it may be difficult to determine which institution—Congress or the President—instills more confidence, the Supreme Court is clearly the institution whose actions elicit the least amount of popular trust. Thus, both in terms of

Table 4.

RANK ORDER DISTRIBUTIONS OF THE CONFIDENCE IN

CONGRESS, THE PRESIDENCY, AND THE SUPREME COURT[a]

	Confidence Rank				
Institution	First	Second	Third	Percent[b]	N
Congress	45%	39%	15%	99	2566
Presidency	46	43	11	100	2566
Supreme Court	9	18	74	101	2566
Percent	100%	100%	100%		
N=	2566	2566	2566		

a. The following items are utilized in measuring levels of institu-
    tional confidence:

    Thinking again about the branches of the national government
    in Washington, in which branch do you have the most faith and
    confidence--the Presidency, the Congress, or the Supreme
    Court?

    Which branch do you have the least faith and confidence in--
    the Presidency, the Congress, or the Supreme Court?

    These two items indicate the respondent's first and third (last)
    ranks; with these ranks thus determined, the "residual" institu-
    tion automatically occupies the second position.

b. Total percentages do not equal 100% due to rounding. Cases
    involving tied ranks or missing data have been deleted in this
    table.

SOURCE: Comparative State Elections Project, University of North
         Carolina.

saliency and confidence, the Supreme Court is literally the "third branch" of the federal government.

We have now defined some of the parameters of the public's cognitive and affective image of Congress and the presidency. We move, at this point, to a more intensive analysis of the characteristics, attitudes, and behavior of supporters of congressional and presidential leadership.

CONGRESSIONAL AND PRESIDENTIAL CONSTITUENCIES

Despite the classical concern of social scientists with political leadership, few empirical studies of mass belief systems have attempted to explore the nature of leader-follower relations. Our present knowledge regarding the bases for an individual's preference for a specific form of political authority or political structure consists largely of speculation, conventional wisdom, some well-reasoned arguments, and a small measure of empirical propositions. The lacunae in the studies of institutional preferences is especially acute with respect to the analysis of supporters of legislative and executive power. The extent of our knowledge in this latter area is almost totally dependent upon what inferences can be drawn from diverse studies of individual governmental structures and a variety of unrelated political orientations.

This segment of the paper will examine the characteristics, attitudes and political involvement of supporters of legislative and executive leadership. The bases for this exploratory rest on a national survey conducted in December, 1968.[4]

The following sequence of survey items is utilized in the measurement of individual preferences for either congressional or presidential leadership in policy-making: Some people think that the President ought to have the major responsibility in making policy while other people think that Congress ought to have the major responsibility. I'd like to ask you what you think.

1. First of all, in making the nation's foreign policy, whom do you think should have the major responsibility—the President, Congress, or both about equal?

2. What about in making the nation's policy in economic or welfare laws—whom do you think should have the major responsibility—the President, Congress, or both about equal?

3. Finally, in policy dealing with racial problems—whom do you think should have the major responsibility—the President, Congress, or both about equal?

Table 5 presents the marginal distribution of leadership preferences within the American public. As the table clearly illustrates, Congress—not the presidency—is the institution which the electorate prefers to dominate in the formation of national policy. Even in the area of foreign policy— long the private domain of presidential leadership—a greater proportion of the electorate favor congressional to presidential leadership. These findings seem to challenge the premise held by some (Sigel, 1966), that the populace prefers presidential, in contrast to congressional, leadership in public policy.[5]

Although we are primarily concerned with individual preferences for either legislative or executive leadership, we have utilized a three-fold classification of policy-making prescriptions. We feel that this tripartite division in leadership prescriptions is preferable to a dichotomization of such prescriptions, in that it more effectively isolates those with distinct institutional predilections (i.e., institutional-support publics). Allowing persons only two response alternatives—policy leadership on the part of Congress or the President—has the all too common result of forcing

Table 5.

POLICY LEADERSHIP PRESCRIPTIONS WITHIN THE AMERICAN PUBLIC

	Foreign Policy	Economic Policy	Racial Policy
President	15%	7%	11%
Equal	61	60	65
Congress	24	33	25
Percent[a]	100%	100%	101%
N=	1395	1377	1383

a. Total percentages do not equal 100% due to rounding.

individuals who possess no explicit opinion,[6] or who are ambivalent, to express an institutional choice. While excluding from analysis that segment of the populace without definite institutional preferences naturally reduces the sample size, we believe that this truncation will produce a clearer synthesis of those with explicit leadership predilections and, therefore, simplify and sharpen our analysis of institutional constituencies. Thus, we have decided to confine our attention to that sizeable segment of the public which expresses a preference for policy leadership on the part of Congress or the presidency.

The trichotomization of institutional preferences ("Congress-both about equal-President") depresses the strength of some of the observed correlations. Yet, the inclusion of a variable category for those expressing a predilection for collaborative decision-making does not significantly alter the nature nor the degree of association among the variables. Finally, all of the relationships reported tend to survive the introduction of "control variables."[7]

Table 6.

PUBLIC PRESCRIPTIONS FOR LEADERSHIP

IN THE FORMATION OF PUBLIC POLICY[a]

Prescription	Percent
Congress	27%
Presidency	9
Both about equal	64
Percent	100%
N=	1339

a. Cases involving missing data on two or more policy prescriptions have been deleted in this table.

Table 7.

ATTITUDES TOWARD CONGRESS ON THE PART OF PERSONS EXPRESSING

AN INSTITUTIONAL PREFERENCE[a]

Attitude Toward Congress	Institutional Preference		Gamma
	Presidency	Congress	
Congressional Leadership			
better now	17% (18)	23% (77)	
about the same	72 (78)	70 (234)	.21
worse now	11 (12)	6 (21)	
Legislative Oversight			
agree strongly	30% (32)	51%(181)	
agree somewhat	41 (43)	32 (113)	.34
disagree somewhat	20 (21)	13 (47)	
disagree strongly	9 (9)	4 (14)	
Legislative Cooperation			
agree strongly	14% (15)	5% (18)	
agree somewhat	23 (24)	7 (26)	-.42
disagree somewhat	33 (36)	36 (129)	
disagree strongly	31 (33)	51 (183)	

a. The exact wording of the questions are:

> Compared with what we have produced in the past do you feel our present leadership in Congress, both the House of Representatives and the Senate, is now better, worse, or about the same as we have produced in the past?

> Congress should serve as a watchdog over the President and his executive agencies.

> Congress should always cooperate with the President and not oppose his legislative proposals.

We have taken those responses which express the same institutional preference in any two or more policy areas as an indication of an individual's predilection for either legislative or executive leadership. We feel that the conceptual proximity and empirical association among these policy leadership prescriptions are sufficient to justify this procedure for the definition of institutional constituencies.[8] It is also our belief that this classification process successfully eliminates those who actually have no definite views on the issue of whether congressional or presidential influence should dominate the policy-making process. The results of this classification procedure reveal that approximately three-fifths of the public has no well-defined position on the matter—that is, they show no commitment to either legislative or executive leadership in the formation of public policy; the remainder of the sample split 3 to 1 in favor of congressional leadership (Table 6). Although the size of the President's constituency seems small when compared with the legislative public, we should not underestimate the opportunity and potential of the Chief Executive for summoning broader popular support by invoking the symbols of the office.

It is not surprising, in light of their institutional attachments, for advocates of legislative and presidential leadership to have divergent views of Congress and its role in the political process (Table 7). Presidents frequently bemoan the lack of legislative cooperation on the part of Congress and the penchant of congressmen for the detailed surveillance of executive agencies; presidential partisans appear to take similar positions. Promoters of presidential dominance are more inclined to assert the need for consistent congressional cooperation with the President's legislative proposals and to reject the necessity for legislative oversight of the executive branch. Supporters of presidential leadership are also more likely than their congressional counterparts to hold negative feelings toward a major sector of resistance to executive influence—the legislative leadership. Thus, when mobilized, these two institutional publics are apt to divide over issues concerning the leadership capacity and legislative obligations of Congress.

PARTY IDENTIFICATION AND THE IMPACT OF INCUMBENCY

An attitudinal construct of proven importance in the determination of political attitudes and electoral behavior is party identification (Campbell et al., 1964). Party attachments influence political orientations by providing the person with "cues" which signal particular evaluative responses to various political elements. Clearly, the complexity of politics forces citizens to rely upon such relatively simple techniques as partisan affiliation for assessing what cannot, by its very nature, become matters of personal knowledge. The affective connotations which accompany identification with a political party are especially influential in structuring perceptions of candidates:

> Even those who are not highly partisan have some image—no matter how vague and general—of the two major parties. Undoubtedly, they must carry this image with them when evaluating the candidates. The candidate thus is hardly ever seen just as an individual to whom voters may respond or on whom they may project as they see fit. Rather, he stands both for himself and for his party, and often the image is intensely interwoven [Sigel, 1964: 496].

Table 8.

THE POLITICAL PARTY IDENTIFICATIONS OF PERSONS

EXPRESSING AN INSTITUTIONAL PREFERENCE

Party Affiliation	Institutional Preference	
	Presidency	Congress
Republican	30%	35%
Independent	17	18
Democrat	53	48
	———	———
Percent[a]	100%	101%
N=	111	348
Gamma = .10		

a. Percentages do not equal 100% due to rounding.

Party identification also appears to effect orientations toward political institutions. For example, Kenneth Dolbeare and Philip Hammond have observed that there is a party-based component to attitudes toward the Supreme Court. Dolbeare and Hammond (1968: 29), conclude that "for the great majority of people, party—as party, not as a surrogate for ideology or socio-economic status—is, together with presidential incumbency, the dominant source of cues for attitudes toward the Court."

If people view the Court from the perspectives of Republicans and Democrats, it seems reasonable to expect party identification to function in a similar capacity with respect to governmental structures that are more overtly partisan. Furthermore, the influence of partisanship on institutional preferences should be most pronounced during periods of "divided government," such as confronted the nation as a result of the 1968 elections; at these times, the partisan difference between Congress and the President would be most visible.

Therefore, there is some reason to anticipate that supporters of presidential and congressional leadership differ from one another in terms of partisan affiliation. The basis for this argument rests on the belief that individuals will prefer institutional leadership on the part of the political structure whose current partisan membership is consistent with their own party identifications. Since Republicans recovered the White House in 1968, but once again failed to capture party control of Congress, we might expect that Republicans would have a greater predilection for executive, in contrast to legislative, power. On the other hand, Democratic control of Congress should incline Democratic party adherents to favor congressional leadership in the formation of public policy. Thus, we might expect a greater predominance of Republicans within the presidential constituency than among persons favoring congressional leadership; Democrats, in contrast, should constitute a greater proportion of those supporting legislative dominance in the formation of public policy.

As Table 8 illustrates, there is only a slight difference between the party affiliations of congressional supporters and those who advocate presidential leadership. Moreover, the relationship is not in the expected direction. There is a larger proportion of Democrats among those who feel that the President should maintain the primary responsibility for the formation of public policy. Thus, supporters of presidential and congressional leadership are "partisans" in purely an institutional sense.

The argument might be advanced that leadership predilections mirror attitudes toward the incumbent President—the personification of the office of the presidency. Hence, institutional orientations may reflect little more than popular satisfaction/dissatisfaction with the man in the White House. We would expect, therefore, that disillusionment with President

Johnson would incline individuals to prefer congressional to presidential leadership. In a similar vein, we might expect that those who failed to see their presidential candidate elected—Humphrey and Wallace voters—would be more apt to support congressional rather than executive leadership in the formation of public policy. Neither of these potentially explanatory hypotheses is supported by the data (Table 9); controlling for the possible confounding effects of party identification on the evaluations of President Johnson and on the 1968 presidential preferences of institutional partisans does little to improve the negligible zero-order associations.

Table 9.

INSTITUTIONAL PARTISANSHIP AND INCUMBANCY EFFECTS

Indicator of Incumbancy	Institutional Preference	
	Presidency	Congress
Evaluation of President Johnson		
Excellent	12% (14)	12% (42)
Pretty Good	43 (48)	39 (141)
Only Fair	37 (41)	35 (152)
Poor	9 (10)	15 (52)
1968 Presidential Vote		
Richard M. Nixon	48% (40)	42% (121)
Hubert H. Humphrey	40 (33)	47 (136)
George Wallace	11 (9)	11 (31)

THE SOCIO-ECONOMIC CHARACTERISTICS OF INSTITUTIONAL PARTISANS

Supporters of congressional and presidential leadership appear to differ in their socio-demographic characteristics (Table 10). For example, those

Table 10.

SOCIO-DEMOGRAPHIC CHARACTERISTICS OF PERSONS EXPRESSING

AN INSTITUTIONAL PREFERENCE

Characteristics	Institutional Preference		Gamma
	Presidency	Congress	
Education			
More than 12th grade	31% (35)	33%(119)	
12th grade	30 (34)	32 (116)	.07
Less than 12th grade	39 (44)	34 (123)	
Age			
50 and over	32% (36)	44%(159)	
35 - 49	34 (38)	29 (106)	.20
21 - 34	35 (39)	27 (96)	
Income			
10,000 and over	38% (46)	37%(126)	
5,000 - 9,999	39 (42)	42 (145)	.02
0 - 4,999	24 (26)	21 (72)	
Race			
White	86% (98)	92%(334)	.33
None-white	14 (16)	8 (27)	
Occupation			
Professional and White Collar	30% (29)	44%(135)	.30
Skilled and Unskilled Workers	70 (68)	56 (171)	
Sex			
Male	45% (52)	63%(229)	.35
Female	55 (62)	37 (133)	

who express a preference for congressional leadership tend to be males and generally older than those with a predilection for presidential power. In addition, supporters of legislative leadership are more likely than advocates of executive leadership to be employed in the higher status occupations. Despite such clear demographic distinctions, institutional adherents differ only marginally with respect to income or level of education. We might expect that the unpopularity of the President-elect in 1968—Richard M. Nixon—among racial minorities[9] would make non-whites less enthusiastic than whites about executive leadership in the formation of public policy. This is not, however, the case. Non-whites are decisively more likely to favor policy-making leadership on the part of the Chief Executive, even in the area of racial problems.

These differences in the socio-economic profiles of the congressional and presidential publics probably affects the potential of these institutional constituencies for political involvement and mobilization. For example, it is frequently observed that men are more likely than women to participate in politics; that political participation increases with age and socio-economic status; and that Whites are more participative than Blacks (Milbrath, 1965). This would seem to suggest that the congressional constituency is more likely than the presidential public to engage in the defense of institutional prerogatives; we will return to this point at a later stage in the analysis.

ATTITUDES TOWARD POLITICAL REPRESENTATION AND CONGRESSIONAL AND PRESIDENTIAL PARTISANSHIP

Congress has often been accused, perhaps unjustly, of being "oriented toward local needs and small-town ways of thought" (Huntington, 1965: 16). A similar point is made by James Rosenau, who concludes that the individual congressman typically reflects "segmental" orientations, while other national leaders, like the President, have what he terms "continental" orientations. What distinguishes the segmentally oriented leaders is that they "give highest priority to subnational concerns" (Rosenau, 1963: 31). The segmental outlook of the Representative may be largely a function of his more provincial origins and characteristics (Hacker, 1961: 539-549), but regardless of its source, the provincialism of Congress appears to be an attribute commonly associated with the legislative process.

The assumed focus of Congress on local concerns is usually contrasted with the purported interest of the President with problems more national in scope. For example, Samuel Huntington (1965: 17) has suggested that the American political system is approaching a "three-way system of representation," wherein the national interest is "represented territorially and functionally in the Presidency," and "particular territorial interests are represented in Congress." Elmer Cornwell (1966: 302) aptly summarizes the argument:

> The Congress represents the nation in terms of local groups and interests, while the President represents it as a whole and particularly its *national* interests and currents of opinion. Congress thus has a vested interest in promoting local claims and ignoring national claims, while the President seeks to emphasize national goals and problems at the expense of parochialism.

In addition, there is some reason to believe that the mass public makes a similar distinction in the respective representational capacities of Congress and the President (Lane, 1962: 147-152).

Thus, we might expect that persons who support congressional leadership do so because they approve of the purported localism of Congress. On the other hand, those who favor executive domination in policy-making may feel that Congress is too parochial in its outlook and should be more "cosmopolitan" in its orientation to political issues. Therefore, we would expect that supporters of congressional leadership would be more likely to believe that the individual congressman should be primarily concerned with his own district, while adherents to executive leadership would more often assert that the Representative's responsibility is to the nation as a whole. This argument is voided in a most pronounced fashion: A slightly greater proportion of those advocating presidential leadership, in contrast to congressional, prescribe a local focus for their congressman (Table 11).

There is, however, a significant difference between advocates of congressional and presidential leadership in terms of the style of representation. For instance, about 45 percent of those supporting leadership on the part of the President believe that "when there is a conflict between what a U.S. Representative feels is best and what the people in his district want," the congressman should be guided by his conscience rather than adhering to the opinions of his constituents; about one-third of those supporting legislative leadership express an identical prescription. Consistent with their preferences for a "trustee" style of representation, advocates of presidential leadership are more inclined than congressional partisans to believe that a representative should "vote his conscience."

We also observe that those with a predilection for congressional leadership are more likely than those with a preference for presidential leadership to select the Tribune interpretation of the congressman's role.[10]

Table 11.

PRESCRIPTIONS FOR THE FOCUS OF REPRESENTATION

ON THE PART OF PERSONS EXPRESSING AN INSTITUTIONAL PREFERENCE[a]

Prescription	Institutional Preference	
	Presidency	Congress
Nation	22%	21%
Both equal	44	56
District	34	24
Percent[b]	100%	101%
N=	113	359
Gamma = -.12		

a. The exact wording of the question is:

> Do you think your representative should be concerned primarily with his district, or with the nation as a whole, or with both about equal?

b. Total percentages do not equal 100% due to rounding.

Table 12.

ATTITUDES TOWARD THE STYLE OF REPRESENTATION

ON THE PART OF PERSONS EXPRESSING AN INSTITUTIONAL PREFERENCE[a]

Attitude	Institutional Preference		Gamma
	Presidency	Congress	
Primary Role Prescription			
tribune	71% (78)	85%(274)	
ritualist inventor broker mentor-communicator	29 (32)	15 (50)	.38
Style of Representation			
follow conscience	45% (48)	33%(114)	
depends (volunteered)	16 (17)	17 (58)	-.22
follow district opinion	39 (42)	51 (177)	
Congressmen Should Vote Their Conscience			
agree strongly	23% (24)	20% (67)	
agree somewhat	38 (41)	20 (68)	-.29
disagree somewhat	26 (28)	28 (96)	
disagree strongly	14 (15)	32 (109)	
Congressmen Should Help Constituents			
agree strongly	56% (61)	66%(230)	
agree somewhat	39 (42)	30 (104)	.18
disagree strongly	4 (4)	2 (8)	
disagree strongly	1 (2)	3 (9)	

Table 12. (continued)

From this perspective, the representative is viewed as a discoverer, re-
flector, and advocate of popular needs and demands. A qualitative exam-
ination of the content of Tribune prescriptions suggests that individuals
employing this role orientation expect a significant degree of *personal
representation* on the part of their congressman. Thus, persons expressing
a preference for legislative leadership in the formation of national policy
are more likely than those who advocate presidential leadership to believe
that the congressman should be the people's elected agent.

THE POTENTIAL FOR MOBILIZATION:
POLITICAL INVOLVEMENT AND INSTITUTIONAL SUPPORTERS

We have now compared the congressional and presidential constituencies with respect to several socio-demographic and political characteristics; we turn, at this point, to a consideration of the capacity of the
institutional constituencies for political mobilization. Congressional supporters appear to display a greater potential for political involvement than
those who express a preference for presidential leadership (Table 13). For
one thing, advocates of legislative dominance seem to have accepted the
tenet that it is the duty of the citizen to actively participate in politics.
Specifically, congressional partisans are more likely than those with a

Table 13.

PREDISPOSITIONS FOR POLITICAL INVOLVEMENT ON THE PART OF PERSONS
EXPRESSING AN INSTITUTIONAL PREFERENCE[a]

Predisposition	Institutional Preference		Gamma
	Presidency	Congress	
Leave Issues to Elected Officials			
agree strongly	10% (11)	4% (15)	
agree somewhat	20 (22)	12 (42)	-.19
disagree somewhat	21 (23)	27 (95)	
disagree strongly	50 (55)	57 (200)	
Shouldn't Vote If You Don't Care About Outcome			
agree strongly	36% (40)	32%(114)	
agree somewhat	25 (28)	19 (67)	-.14
disagree somewhat	21 (23)	20 (70)	
disagree strongly	19 (21)	29 (104)	
People Don't Have a Say in What Government Does			
agree strongly	15% (17)	12% (42)	
agree somewhat	33 (37)	17 (61)	-.28
disagree somewhat	29 (32)	34 (122)	
disagree strongly	23 (26)	37 (131)	
Officials Don't Care What I Think			
agree strongly	17% (19)	11% (39)	
agree somewhat	27 (30)	23 (80)	-.17
disagree somewhat	35 (39)	38 (133)	
disagree strongly	21 (23)	28 (99)	

Table 13. (continued)

Voting Is Only Way to Have a
 Say in Government

agree strongly	34% (38)	49%(171)	
agree somewhat	44 (49)	28 (99)	
disagree somewhat	13 (15)	16 (58)	.16
disagree strongly	9 (9)	7 (24)	

Local Elections Aren't Important

agree strongly	7% (8)	7% (15)	
agree somewhat	15 (17)	8 (29)	
disagree somewhat	29 (33)	28 (98)	-.24
disagree strongly	48 (53)	60 (212)	

Politics is Complicated

agree strongly	47% (53)	37%(130)	
agree somewhat	36 (41)	43 (153)	
disagree somewhat	11 (12)	14 (49)	-.16
disagree strongly	6 (7)	7 (24)	

a. The exact wording of the questions are:

It would be better if most people didn't worry about political issues, but left them for elected officials.

If a person doesn't care how an election comes out he shouldn't vote in it.

People like me don't have any say about what the government does

I don't think that public officials care what people like me think.

Voting is the only way that people like me can have a say about how the government runs things.

A good many local elections are not important enough to bother about.

Sometimes politics and government seem so complicated that a person can't really understand what's going on.

predilection for executive leadership to believe that local elections are important, that a person should vote—even if he has little interest in the electoral outcome—and that individuals should be concerned about political issues, rather than leaving the resolution of such issues to the designs of public officials.

Trust in the responsiveness of the political system also appears to be more frequent within the congressional constituency. For instance, those expressing a preference for legislative, in contrast to executive, policy-making leadership are more inclined to believe that individuals do have a "say" in what the government does; they also express a slightly greater willingness to believe that public officials have an interest in their opinions. In addition to their confidence in the receptivity of political elites to popular opinion and their emphasis on the civic responsibilities of voting, congressional supporters are more likely to express feelings of personal political competence: Congressional partisans less frequently acknowledge difficulty in understanding "politics and government."

Advocates of congressional leadership, apparently, realize their potential for political activity. For example, they are more likely than those expressing a preference for executive leadership to have voted in all national elections between 1964 and 1968 (Table 14). Legislative partisans are also more participative with respect to a variety of political activities related to Congress (Table 15). Specifically, supporters of Congress are more likely than adherents of presidential leadership to have attended a rally or meeting for a congressional candidate, to have communicated with their Representative, and to be politically informed. In conclusion, then, congressional partisans display a greater propensity for political involvement and mobilization than is found within the presidential constituency.

The greater communication between constituent and Representative within the congressional constituency suggests that congressmen are more likely to "hear" from those who take the side of Congress in its struggle with the Executive over the formation of public policy. Therefore, if the congressman "reads" constituent mail as an adequate barometer of district sentiment, as many undoubtedly do, he may very well receive an exaggerated impression of popular support for greater legislative involvement in policy-making. This finding also appears to question the common strategy of Presidents in appealing to citizens to "write their Congressman" on his (the President's) behalf. His pleas for grass-root involvement seem more likely to stir to action the more politically informed and motivated congressional partisans, rather than presidential advocates.

Table 14.

THE ELECTORAL PARTICIPATION ON THE PART OF PERSONS EXPRESSING
AN INSTITUTIONAL PREFERENCE: 1964 TO 1968

Electoral Participation	Institutional Preference		Gamma
	Presidency	Congress	
1964 Election			
voted	67% (76)	79%(280)	
didn't vote	33 (38)	22 (80)	.27
1966 Election			
voted	59% (61)	71%(245)	
didn't vote	41 (42)	29 (101)	.25
1968 Election			
voted	74% (84)	83%(299)	
didn't vote	26 (30)	17 (62)	.26

Table 15.

POLITICAL INVOLVEMENT IN CONGRESSIONAL ACTIVITIES ON THE PART

OF PERSONS EXPRESSING AN INSTITUTIONAL PREFERENCE

Indicant of Involvement	Institutional Preference		Gamma
	Presidency	Congress	
Interest in Congressional Campaign			
very interested	28% (32)	36%(127)	
fairly interested	34 (39)	33 (116)	.11
slightly interested	29 (32)	20 (71)	
not interested	9 (10)	11 (40)	
Political Information (Knowledge of Party Control)			
yes	74% (82)	86%(310)	.40
no	28 (31)	14 (50)	
Campaigned for a Congressional Candidate			
yes	12% (14)	13% (47)	.06
no	88 (100)	87 (312)	
Attended a Rally for a Congressional Candidate			
yes	32% (37)	38%(137)	.13
no	68 (77)	62 (222)	
Financial Contribution to a Congressional Campaign			
yes	17% (19)	24% (86)	.22
no	83 (95)	76 (273)	

Table 15. (continued)

Sent Communication to
  Congressman

yes	38% (43)	54%(194)	
no	62 (71)	46 (166)	.31

Personal Visit with
  Congressman

yes	19% (21)	17% (61)	
no	81 (93)	83 (298)	-.06

Attention to Media Reports
  about Congressman

often	33% (37)	29%(103)	
not often	34 (38)	49 (173)	.07
not at all	33 (36)	22 (76)	

Received Communication
  from Congressman

yes	74% (84)	80%(288)	
no	26 (29)	20 (72)	.17

SUMMARY: THE AUTONOMOUS PRESIDENT, THE RESPONSIVE CONGRESS

Admittedly, the findings presented in this paper fall short of providing a detailed profile of presidential and congressional constituencies; further, the evidence from our survey is by no means conclusive, nor can we be certain that our inferences are not timebound. With these caveats in mind, we will hazard a few generalizations based on the findings.

Perhaps the most obvious conclusion to be drawn from the preceding analysis is that although Congress does not hold a revered place in the public's cognitive map of the political world, it fares far better in its competition with the President than some commentaries suggest. Generally speaking, people are decisively more attentive to presidential—rather than congressional—affairs. Yet, Congress is more likely to be perceived as having a "great effect" on a person's life, and three-quarters of those with a definite institutional preference believe that Congress should have the leading role in forming public policy.

Demographically speaking, advocates of legislative leadership tend to be white, male, and generally older than those with a predilection for presidential leadership; they are also more likely to be employed in the higher status occupations. These correlates of institutional preferences correspond to differences in participation between support publics. Those who favor legislative leadership in policy-making are more likely to expect the congressman to advocate constituent causes and to follow district opinion, even "when there is a conflict between what a U.S. Representative feels is best and what the people in his district want."

The predispositions for political involvement and the actual electoral activity on the part of those expressing a preference for congressional leadership, when combined with the belief that constituent opinion—in contrast to the dictates of conscience—should direct the congressman's actions, suggest that these individuals claim an active role for themselves in the governing of the polity. These persons appear to have accepted the belief that "it is the business of a democratic state to give the people what they want, to satisfy their stated desires rather than their objective needs (what some wise men conceive their needs to be)" (Spitz, 1958: 92-93). Supporters of presidential leadership, in contrast, are more passive and less worried about popular control over the actions of elected officials.

These differences in mass constituencies are consistent with certain characteristics of these political structures. Specifically, the greater accessibility of Congress, and its responsiveness to citizen mobilization, has greater appeal for the active citizen concerned with personal representation. The autonomous nature of the presidency, on the other hand, attracts the more passive individuals who are less concerned with the independence of political elites from constituent opinion. Advocates of presidential leadership may feel that public officials should follow what they believe to be the proper course of action, undeterred by the constant meddling of constituents, like the decisions made by the President. The essential difference between supporters of congressional and executive leadership, therefore, may hinge on the affective connotations which individuals attach to the simple distinction that Robert Lane's Eastport respondents make between Congress and the presidency: "Congress is responsive; the President is more autonomous" (Lane, 1962: 149).

There are several inferences about the congressional and presidential constituencies which can be drawn from the data. For one thing, the greater attention that individuals pay to the actions of the President provides him with a more captive audience than is supplied to Congress. This may afford the President the opportunity to increase the size of his supportive public beyond the constituency through broad appeals for support. But, not all the advantages accrue to the White House. Because of the differences between the basic supporting publics in terms of information, and political activity, congressional supporters are probably more easily and effectively mobilized in the defense of legislative powers and prerogatives.

CONGRESSIONAL AND PRESIDENTIAL PARTISANS: OUTLOOK FOR THE 1970s

Although few institutions or public officials are likely to be spared from the decline in public confidence and esteem resulting from the "Watergate fallout," the presidency may be the hardest hit since it has been the only major governmental structure which has *not* experienced any rise in public confidence since 1972 (Senate Subcommittee on Intergovernmental Relations, 1973: 35). It may be an exaggeration, however, to attribute this decline solely to the present tenure of Richard Nixon. This does not deny the impact which President Nixon's receding popularity may have on support for presidential leadership in the formation of public policy. Certainly, the President's "political" actions (e.g., impoundments) may have soured some advocates of presidential leadership, and his handling of the Watergate investigation may have made still others suspicious of presidential power. Yet, our findings suggest that dissatisfaction with the incumbent president has only a slight effect on policy-making prescriptions. Perhaps the public's attitude toward the isolation and independence of political institutions and elites will be of greater significance: The autonomy of the presidency itself may lead to decreased support for presidential leadership in public policy.

The perceived independence of political elites appears to be under question, if not attack, by the American public. A report based upon a recent national survey of attitudes toward the functioning of government, commissioned by the Senate Subcommittee on Intergovernmental Affairs of the United States Congress (1973), suggests that a major source of popular discontent is the perceived unresponsiveness of political institutions. For instance, the third most frequently cited reason for a lack of confidence in the federal government—only "corruption" and "Watergate" were mentioned more often—is the "distance" of government and its "unresponsiveness" (19 percent); the second most frequently prescribed remedy for declining confidence is for public officials to become more sensitive to the needs and demands of the citizenry (27 percent). Moreover, the public appears unwilling to accept this isolation as a natural state-of-affairs. "But even considering themselves to be imperfect participants in the democratic process," the report concludes, "they are eager to participate, to work for change, to be made influential individuals in a collective effort to diffuse power and engage the people in its exercise" (Senate Subcommittee on Intergovernmental Relations, 1973: X). Increased public support since 1968 for congressional oversight of the executive branch (a 12 percent increase) may reflect the American electorate's rising apprehension about the autonomous functioning of political structures like the presidency.

With respect to the other institutions of the federal government, Congress may suffer less from the popular concern for governmental responsiveness because Congress is the national political structure which is most susceptible to citizen involvement and mobilization. In fact, Congress may actually derive some benefit from such concern, in that individuals may come to focus greater attention on the legislative process; thus, the saliency of Congress may be enhanced significantly. Clearly, since 1968 there has been an increased amount of public interest in congressional politics as evidenced by the fact that participation in congressional elections has almost doubled with respect to such activities as visiting or talking with congressmen, campaigning for a congressional candidate, and making a financial contribution to a congressional campaign (Senate Subcommittee on Intergovernmental Relations, 1973: 256).

In conclusion, public concern for the responsiveness of political institutions would seem to portend waning popular enthusiasm for presidential leadership in the formation of public policy. Although support for congressional policy-making leadership would seem likely to rise with declining membership in the presidential constituency, we cannot be certain that this will occur. It is also quite possible that presidential defections will only increase the proportion of the public without an institutional preference. Declining public confidence may also serve to diminish the size of the congressional constituency, further increasing the proportion of individuals indifferent to either presidential or congressional leadership. Yet, if the relationships which we have observed in the 1968 data between active interest in congressional affairs, preference for responsive political elites, and leadership predilections continue to persist, we would expect the ranks of the congressional constituency to swell.

NOTES

1. The data presented in this paper pertaining to institutional supports (i.e., impact, saliency, and confidence) is based on a subset of a national sample survey conducted in late 1968. This national sample was developed from 14 separate samples—13 individual state samples and one sample for the balance for the continental United States including the District of Columbia, less Alaska and Hawaii. The 13 states which were individually sampled were: Alabama, California, Florida, Illinois, Louisiana, Massachusetts, Minnesota, New York, North Carolina, Ohio, Pennsylvania, South Dakota, and Texas. The sample subset utilized in this exploratory analysis is composed of the sample of the remaining 35 states and a sample from the state of California, the only state in which questionnaire items on institutional orientations were included in the survey instrument. Since the data were acquired for strictly exploratory purposes, it was felt that it would be sufficient, and much less costly, to obtain data from a known and statistically describable subset of the nation. Thus, our findings are, at best, only suggestive of the true parameters of the national populace. For further information on the sampling design, see James Prothro (ed.) The 1968 Election, (forthcoming). All the N's reported in this paper are weighted.

2. American Institute of Public Opinion, November, 1965.

3. A national "pre-Watergate" survey conducted in 1972 indicates slightly greater public trust in the presidency (see the Survey Research Center's 1972 Election Study Codebook). Whether the differences in the findings on institutional confidence reported here and the results of the SRC survey are due to the different types of samples, the different question formats for the two surveys, or represents an actual change in attitudes is difficult to ascertain.

4. For a general description of the survey instrument utilized in this analysis see Roger H. Davidson (1970: 648-666). All the N's reported are weighted.

5. The greater support on the part of the mass public for legislative, rather than executive, leadership is consistent with Donald Devine's (1972: 155-163) conclusion that the American people are more likely to endorse congressional, in contrast to presidential, power.

6. Since individuals are generally reluctant to admit that they do not have an

opinion on an issue, the response alternative "both about equal" may provide respondents with a socially acceptable answer if an opinion hasn't really crystallized. As psychologist H. J. Eysenck points out, social approbation

> attaches to the having of opinions on a variety of public issues, and this is probably responsible for the fact that many people express opinions on issues to which in reality they have never given a thought and on which they cannot really be said to have any kind of crystallized opinion at all [H. J. Eysenck, 1963: 60].

Moreover, the scarcity of well-developed attitudes toward political structures appears to be a recurring finding in studies of mass belief systems. For example, Murphy and Tanenhaus (1968: 277) find that approximately 60 percent of the American public lack definite opinions about the performance of the Supreme Court.

7. The control variables utilized in this inquiry are party identification, education, income, and race.

8. The following are the intercorrelations (gamma) along the policy leadership prescriptions:

	Foreign Policy	Economic Policy	Racial Policy
Foreign Policy	1.00		
Economic Policy	.61	1.00	
Racial Policy	.64	.80	1.00

9. President Nixon received only about 10 percent of the non-White vote in 1968.

10. For a discussion of the various role prescriptions that emerge from an analysis of popular descriptions of the job of the representative, see Roger Davidson (1970: 652-659).

REFERENCES

CAMPBELL, A., P. E. CONVERSE, W. E. MILLER, and D. E. STOKES (1964) The American Voter. New York: John Wiley.

CONVERSE, P. E. (1962) "Information flow and the stability of partisan attitudes." Public Opinion Quarterly 26: 578-599.

CORNWELL, E. E., Jr. (1966) Presidential Leadership of Public Opinion. Bloomington: Indiana Univ.

--- (1959) "Presidential news: The expanding public image." Journalism Quarterly 36: 275-283.

CRONIN, T. E. (1970) "The textbook presidency and political science." Paper presented: 66th Annual Meeting of the American Political Science Association.

DAVIDSON, R. H. (1970) "Public prescriptions for the job of congressman." Midwest Journal of Political Science 14: 648-666.

DEVINE, D. J. (1972) The Political Culture of the United States. Boston: Little, Brown.

DOLBEARE, K. M. (1967) "The public views the Supreme Court," pp. 194-212 in H. Jacob (ed.) Law, Politics, and the Federal Courts. Boston: Little, Brown.

——, and P. E. HAMMOND (1968) "The political party basis of attitudes toward the Supreme Court." Public Opinion Quarterly 32, 1: 16-29.

EASTON, D. and J. DENNIS (1969) Children In the Political System. New York: McGraw-Hill.

EYSENCK, H. J. (1963) The Psychology of Politics. London: Routedge and Kegan Paul Ltd.

GREENSTEIN, F. I. (1965) Children and Politics. New Haven: Yale Univ.

HACKER, A. (1961) "The elected and the annointed." American Political Science Review 55: 539-549.

HARRIS, L. (1972) "U.S. confidence in leaders continues at a low level." The Washington Post (November 13): A7.

HUNTINGTON, S. P. (1965) "Congressional response to the twentieth century," pp. 5-31 in D. B. Truman (ed.) The Congress and America's Future. Englewood Cliffs, New Jersey: Prentice Hall.

JAMES, D. B. (1969) The Contemporary Presidency. New York: Pegasus.

KOENIG, L. W. (1964) The Chief Executive. New York: Harcourt, Brace and World.

LANE, R. E. (1962) Political Ideology. New York: Free Press.

McCONNELL, G. (1964) The Modern Presidency. New York: St. Martin's Press.

MILBRATH, L. W. (1965) Political Participation. Chicago: Rand McNally.

MILLER, A. (1972) "Political issues and trust in government: 1964-1970." Paper presented: 68th Annual Meeting of the American Political Science Association.

MURPHY, W. F. and J. TANENHAUS (1969) "Constitutional courts and political representation," pp. 541-554 in M. N. Danielson and W. F. Murphy (eds.) Modern American Democracy: Readings. New York: Holt, Rinehart and Winston.

——— (1968) "Public opinion and the United States Supreme Court." Law and Society II: 273-303.

NEUSTADT, R. E. (1961) Presidential Power. New York: Pegasus.

ROSENAU, J. N. (1963) National Leadership and Foreign Policy. Princeton: Princeton Univ.

SIGEL, R. S. (1966) "Image of the American presidency—part II of an exploration into popular views of presidential power." Midwest Journal of Political Science 10: 123-137.

——— (1964) "Effect of partisanship on the perception of political candidates." Public Opinion Quarterly 28: 483-496.

SPITZ, D. (1958) "Power Personality: The appeal to the 'right man' in democratic states." American Political Science Review 52: 84-97.

Senate Subcommittee on Intergovernmental Relations, Committee of Governmental Operations (1973) A Survey of Public Attitudes. Washington, D.C.: Government Printing Office.

WASBY, S. L. (1970) The Impact of the United States Supreme Court. Homewood: Dorsey Press.

GLENN R. PARKER, an Assistant Professor of Political Science at Miami University, served as the 1973 coordinator for Senator Howard Metzenbaum in his Oxford primary campaign. Dr. Parker's research interests include public opinion, methodology, electoral behavior, and the legislative process; his most recent publications are "Congress and the American Public: Some Findings on the Correlates of Congressional Evaluations" prepared for inclusion in a forthcoming volume of Jack Dennis' (ed.) Public Support for the Political System *and a book review of* Congressmen's Voting Decisions *by John W. Kingdon, in the November 1974 issue of* Journal of Politics.